THE DAY TRADING COUNSELOR

A Psychological Guide to Discipline, Risk, Revenge Trading & Prop Firm Survival

CHRIS LLOYD
2026

COPYRIGHT & DISCLAIMER

This book is for educational and informational purposes only. It is not financial, investment, legal, tax, or mental-health advice. Futures trading and leveraged financial products involve substantial risk, including the possible loss of capital. No strategy, psychological technique, or risk-management framework guarantees profits.

Prop-firm programs differ in their rules, drawdown calculations, news restrictions, payout requirements, and other conditions. Rules can change. Always read and verify the current rules of the specific program you are using.

Never risk money needed for essential living expenses. If trading is causing significant distress, compulsive behavior, relationship problems, or interference with daily life, consider speaking with an appropriately qualified professional.

DEDICATION

To every trader who has stared at a losing account and wondered how it happened again.

To the person who knows the rules but sometimes struggles to follow them.

To the trader who has chased losses, oversized, revenge traded, and wondered whether it was time to quit.

And to the families who quietly experience the emotional side of trading alongside the person sitting at the screen.

This book is for the trader who is ready to stop fighting the market and start working on himself.

Most importantly, this book is written from a Christian perspective and is offered with gratitude to Jesus Christ, whose place in my life must remain greater than any financial goal.

AUTHOR'S NOTE

I did not set out to write another book telling traders where to enter a trade. There are already plenty of charts, indicators, strategies, signals, and people promising the perfect setup. I wanted to write about the part of trading that is harder to see: the person behind the chart.

My long-term vision for trading was never to spend my life glued to a desk. I pictured waking up somewhere remote, making a few thoughtful trades, and then going on about life. Trading was supposed to create freedom. What I eventually learned was that the dream of freedom can become a trap if you make the market responsible for providing that freedom immediately.

I have experienced repeated losses. I have revenge traded. I have oversized. I have traded when I needed money. I have thought about trades long after the screen was closed. I have wanted to quit. The hardest realization was not that I didn't know what to do. I knew. The problem was following through when emotion became stronger than the plan.

That is why this book is called The Day Trading Counselor. I am not writing as someone who has discovered a magical way to eliminate losses. I am writing as someone who has learned that the trader must be counseled before the trade can be controlled.

My faith is part of that counseling. I am a follower of Jesus Christ, and I believe God must come first. Trading cannot become my identity, my source of peace, or the thing I believe will finally make me whole.

Trading is a tool. Family is real. Life is real. Faith is real. And the market will still be open tomorrow.

If you are reading this after blowing an account, I want you to know something: the account may be damaged, but the lesson does not have to be wasted. Stop. Step away. Let the revenge leave you. Pray. Spend time with your family. Exercise. Sleep. Review what happened when your mind is clear. Then, if and when you return, come back smaller, slower, and wiser.

TABLE OF CONTENTS

PART I — THE TRADER BEFORE THE TRADE

The Question That Started Everything

Why do traders keep blowing accounts?

That question is the heartbeat of this book.

I have learned that the answer is rarely found in another indicator. It is usually found in the space between what a trader knows and what a trader does when pressure arrives.

Most traders already know the basics. They know they should use a stop. They know they should not revenge trade. They know they should not oversize. They know major news can create dangerous volatility. They know they should stop after reaching a daily loss limit.

Knowing is not the same as doing.

The difficult part of trading begins after the knowledge is acquired. It begins when the screen is moving, the position is red, the heart is beating faster, and the mind starts negotiating with the rules.

That is where this book lives.

I am not writing to shame the trader who has blown an account.

I am writing to help that trader understand the pattern well enough to interrupt it.

Every trading lesson eventually comes back to the same question: what will you do when the market does something you did not expect? A plan is easy to admire while everything is working. The real test begins when the trade moves against you, when you miss the move, when you are up more than expected, or when the day begins differently than you imagined.

That is why this section is not just about market knowledge. It is about creating a response before the emotion arrives. Decide what you will do when the condition appears. Decide what you will not do. Put the decision somewhere you can see it.

I have learned that the strongest trader is not necessarily the trader who feels no emotion. The stronger trader is the one who can notice the emotion without allowing it to make the decision. Fear can be present and you can still follow the plan. Frustration can be present and you can still close the platform. Excitement can be present and you can still keep the same size.

The counselor's role is to slow the moment down. Before you ask, “What should I trade?” ask, “What state am I in?” Then ask, “What does my plan require?” If those two answers do not line up, waiting is a legitimate decision.

Remember the larger purpose. Trading is supposed to support a life, not consume it. Keep your priorities visible, keep your risk small enough to think clearly, and keep enough distance from the market to remember that tomorrow will bring another opportunity.

COUNSELOR'S LENS: Write one sentence describing the behavior you want to change. Keep it specific enough that you can recognize it tomorrow.

The Person Behind the Chart

Before you become a trader, you are already a person carrying a life.

You may have a family. You may have bills. You may have a job. You may have experienced layoffs, disappointment, career changes, pressure, or seasons when you had to rebuild. You may be trying to create something better for the people you love.

All of that comes into the trading room with you.

The market does not know what happened to you before you opened the platform, but your nervous system does.

That is why the same chart can produce two completely different decisions from the same trader on two different days.

On Monday you take the stop without hesitation.

On Tuesday you move it.

The chart may be similar. Your internal state is not.

Professional trading begins when you stop pretending that emotions are separate from execution.

THE DEEPER LESSON: Circle the sentence in this section that describes you most closely. That is the behavior worth working on first.

The Market Is Not Your Enemy

The market did not force you to take the extra contract.

It did not force you to remove the stop.

It did not force you to trade after reaching your daily goal.

It did not force you to chase the candle you missed.

The market provided an environment. You made the decision.

That is not a statement of condemnation. It is a statement of freedom.

If the market is responsible for everything, then you are powerless.

If you own your decisions, you can change them.

The first step toward becoming consistent is accepting responsibility without turning responsibility into shame.

PRACTICAL APPLICATION: Before your next trading session, turn this lesson into one written rule. If the rule cannot be

measured, rewrite it.

What This Book Is Really About

This is a trading book, but it is not primarily about entries.

It is about the person who clicks the button.

It is about the emotional sequence before the mistake.

It is about why a loss can feel like an insult.

It is about why a winning streak can be just as dangerous as a losing streak.

It is about why financial pressure can turn a reasonable opportunity into a desperate decision.

It is about why a trader who needs trading to work immediately is operating from a fundamentally different psychological position than a trader who has time to learn.

And it is about how to build a life and a trading process that do not require one trade to save you.

SELF-CHECK: Ask yourself: What would this look like if I were already trading professionally? Then identify one action that matches that answer.

The Reality Check

If you are reading this because you have blown multiple accounts, I want you to pause.

Do not promise yourself that you will simply be more disciplined tomorrow.

Promises made immediately after a blowup are often emotional promises.

Instead, become curious.

What happened?

What did you feel?

What were you trying to accomplish?

When did the original plan disappear?

What did you tell yourself?

What rule did you know you were breaking?

Where did the first bad decision actually occur?

The final loss is not always the beginning of the problem.

Find the beginning.

Leverage Compresses Time

Futures trading can make small price movements feel enormous. Leverage changes the relationship between time and money. A decision that takes two seconds can have financial consequences that feel much larger than the amount of time invested.

That is why futures demand respect.

The faster the market and the larger the position, the less room you have for emotional hesitation.

A trader who wants to think clearly must create enough distance between price movement and emotional reaction to remain capable of following the plan.

The P&L (Profit and Loss) Trap

One of the quickest ways to lose objectivity is to stare at P&L.

The chart says structure.

The P&L says fear.

The chart says the setup remains valid.

The P&L says, "Get out."

The chart says the stop has not been reached.

The P&L says, "Move it."

This is why experienced traders often focus more heavily on price structure and predetermined risk than on the changing dollar number.

Money matters.

But if watching the money causes you to abandon the process, you have allowed the scoreboard to become the strategy.

The Market Will Find Your Weak Spot

If you are impatient, there will be endless periods where nothing happens.

If you are greedy, there will be days when the market moves without you.

If you are afraid, there will be perfectly valid setups.

If you need to be right, there will be trades that prove you wrong immediately.

Trading does not necessarily create these weaknesses. It gives them a microphone.

A New Definition of Success

Success is not a green screenshot.

Success is doing what you said you would do.

If your plan says two trades maximum and you stop after two, that is success.

If your plan says risk one unit and you keep the risk at one unit, that is success.

If you lose while following your rules, you have experienced a controlled loss—not a failure.

This distinction is one of the foundations of professional thinking.

The Lessons Nobody Posts

Social media makes trading look like a collection of entries and payouts.

The hidden curriculum is different.

You must learn to wait.

You must learn to lose.

You must learn to stop.

You must learn to miss a move without chasing it.

You must learn that a profitable trade can be poorly executed.

You must learn that a losing trade can be perfectly executed.

You must learn that your best trading may sometimes look like doing nothing.

Trading and Gambling

Trading becomes gambling when the outcome matters more than the process.

A gambler asks, "How much can I make?"

A professional asks, "What is my defined risk, what is my edge, and what conditions make this trade invalid?"

The difference is not the instrument.

The difference is the relationship with uncertainty.

The First Lesson: Lose Gracefully

You cannot become a consistent trader without becoming comfortable with controlled losses.

A stop is not an insult.

A stop is the price of participating in an uncertain environment.

When you accept that before entering, the stop becomes part of the trade instead of a surprise.

The goal is not to eliminate losses.

The goal is to eliminate unnecessary losses.

The Second Lesson: Stop Winning

One of the hardest lessons is learning to stop when things are going well.

Winning creates confidence. Confidence can create risk expansion. Risk expansion creates mistakes.

A trader who has no winning-day rule can turn a great morning into a terrible afternoon.

Your ability to stop while winning is a form of risk management.

The Third Lesson: Accept Uncertainty

There is no perfect setup.

There is only a setup that meets your criteria under current conditions.

You do not need certainty.

You need a repeatable decision process.

The moment you demand certainty from the market, you begin creating stories to justify your position.

Fear

Fear often appears before the trade.

You hesitate.

You miss the entry.

You enter late.

You take profit too early.

Then the trade moves exactly as expected.

The problem may not be the strategy.

The problem may be that the risk is too large relative to your emotional tolerance.

Reduce the risk until you can execute without your body fighting the decision.

Greed

Greed is not always a desire for luxury.

Sometimes greed is simply refusing to stop.

You hit your target and think there is more.

You make three good trades and think you have figured out the day.

You increase size because you feel momentum.

The professional response to a good day is not necessarily to trade more.

Sometimes the professional response is to protect it.

Ego

Ego says, "I know what the market is going to do."

Humility says, "This is what I believe, and I know I can be wrong."

That small difference can determine whether a trader exits when invalidated or argues with the chart.

Identity

If you call yourself a winner after a green day and a loser after a red day, you have given the market control over your identity.

That is too expensive.

Your account is an account.

You are a person.

Keep those categories separate.

Faith

I am a follower of Jesus Christ, and that matters to how I approach this journey.
My faith reminds me that my identity is not established by money, performance, status, or a trading result.
That gives me a foundation for humility.
When I win, I do not have to become arrogant.
When I lose, I do not have to become ashamed.
I can learn without worshiping the outcome.
For me, trading belongs under a larger framework of stewardship, self-control, honesty, patience, and responsibility.
My faith changes the order of the conversation. Before I ask what the market can give me, I have to remember who I am and what I am responsible for. Trading cannot become the source of my identity, peace, security, or worth. Those are too important to hand over to a fluctuating chart.
As a believer, I want my relationship with God to remain ahead of trading. If I am spending more mental energy chasing a candle than I am spending cultivating my relationship with God, something is out of order. That does not mean trading is wrong. It means trading has to remain in its proper place.
This perspective also changes how I respond to setbacks. A losing day can be painful without becoming a statement about my value. A winning day can be encouraging without becoming proof that I am invincible. Both are temporary. My identity is bigger than a P&L statement.

Counselor's reflection: Before the market opens, ask, "What am I putting first today?" Then ask, "If the market gives me nothing today, can I still have a good day?" If the answer is yes, you have created emotional space that money cannot buy.

PART II — THE ACCOUNT KILLERS

The Phrase Every Trader Understands

There is a phrase that captures the emotional reality of revenge trading: "I need to get my lick back."

The phrase is funny until it costs you an account.

You take a loss.

You feel embarrassed.

You feel cheated.

You tell yourself the next trade will fix it.

That trade is no longer about your setup.

It is about the previous trade.

That is the moment the emotional debt begins.

The Revenge Sequence

Loss.

Frustration.

Urgency.

Lower standards.

Larger size.

Another loss.

Anger.

More size.

Rule violation.

Drawdown violation.

Account gone.

The sequence is predictable.

That is good news.

If the pattern is predictable, you can interrupt it before the final stage.

The important thing is to recognize that revenge rarely announces itself as revenge. It usually arrives disguised as confidence. You tell yourself the next setup is obvious. You tell yourself that you are simply going to make back what you lost. You may even convince yourself that you are following your strategy. But underneath the explanation is urgency. You want the emotional pain of the loss to disappear, and you are asking the next trade to do that job.

That is why the first intervention has to happen before the next entry. Close the platform. Remove the ability to act on the impulse. If you have to physically leave the room, do it. Pray. Talk to your spouse or someone you trust. Exercise. Review something completely unrelated to the market. Search for another investment opportunity. Do anything that reminds you that your financial future is bigger than one chart.

I learned that I did not need to defeat the market after a loss. I needed to defeat the urge to respond immediately. Once the revenge is out of me, I can look at the same market with completely different eyes. The candles did not change. My mind did.

Counselor's question: If you lost money today and nobody knew about it, would you still feel compelled to trade again immediately? If the answer is yes, your next trade may be about emotion rather than opportunity.

The 15-Minute Reset

When you recognize revenge mode, close the platform.

Stand up.

Walk.

Drink water.

Slow your breathing.

Write the facts of the last trade without commentary.

Then ask:

Would I take this trade if the previous trade had never happened?

If the answer is no, the trade is revenge.

Do not take it.

The Deeper Issue

Revenge trading is often less about money than identity.

You are trying to prove that you are not wrong.

You are trying to prove that you are still good at this.

You are trying to erase the feeling of losing.

But no trade can repair your identity.

Only your process can rebuild your confidence.

Why Traders Trade Too Much

Sometimes it is greed.

Sometimes it is boredom.

Sometimes it is fear.

Sometimes it is the need to feel productive.

Trading creates a dangerous illusion: clicking feels like working.

But activity is not productivity.

The best trade may be the one you refuse to take.

Oversizing Is a Psychological Decision

Traders often describe oversizing as a math problem.

It is usually a psychology problem first.

Why did you choose five contracts instead of two?

What did you want the larger size to accomplish?

Were you trying to make more money?

Were you trying to recover?

Were you trying to pass faster?

Were you trying to prove confidence?

The number on the screen is the result of a decision made somewhere inside your mind.

Position size is one of the clearest windows into a trader's emotional state. A trader can say that he is following a strategy, but the number of contracts often tells the real story. When size suddenly increases after a loss, the trader is frequently trying to compress time. He wants the recovery to happen now. When size increases after a winning streak, he may be trying to extend an emotional high.

Professional sizing does the opposite. It creates room for uncertainty. It allows a normal losing trade to remain a normal losing trade. The correct question is not, "How much can I make if this works?" It is, "How much can I lose if I am wrong, and can I remain emotionally stable afterward?"

I want my planned size to feel almost boring. If a position makes my heart race before the trade has even developed, that is useful information. It tells me that the position may be larger than my current psychological capacity. The market does not reward bravery for its own sake.

Counselor's exercise: Write down the size you normally trade, then write down the size at which you begin to feel nervous. Your professional size should be comfortably below the point where fear or excitement begins controlling your decisions.

The Boring Size

Your proper size should be boring.

You should not feel a rush when you enter.

You should not stare at every tick.

You should not feel panic when the trade moves against you normally.

If the position changes your personality, reduce it.

The Daily Trade Limit

Set a maximum number of trades before the session.

Do not wait until you are emotional to create the rule.

For example:

Maximum trades: 3

Maximum consecutive losses: 2

Maximum daily loss: predefined

After reaching the daily objective: stop and review

The exact numbers should fit your account and strategy. The

principle is more important than the specific number: precommit before emotion arrives.

Movement Is Not the Same as Opportunity

News can create extraordinary movement.

That movement attracts traders because movement looks like opportunity.

But fast movement can also mean poor fills, rapid reversals, slippage, and invalidated technical assumptions.

Do not confuse speed with quality.

Build a News Filter

Before every session, know the major scheduled economic events relevant to the market you trade.

If your strategy does not have tested rules for those conditions, do not improvise.

Wait.

Let the initial reaction occur.

Then evaluate whether the market has returned to conditions your strategy understands.

News is not simply a technical event. It is a psychological environment change. A market that was moving in an orderly way can become a completely different market within seconds. That matters because traders tend to keep applying the same expectations to a completely different environment.

The temptation is strongest when a trader believes volatility means opportunity. It does create opportunity, but opportunity and suitability are not the same thing. A move can be enormous and still be a terrible trade for a trader whose account rules, execution speed, or emotional tolerance cannot handle it.

For a trader trying to survive a prop-firm evaluation, protecting the account around major releases can be more valuable than catching a spectacular move. Missing a trade is temporary. Violating a drawdown rule can end the evaluation.

My preference is to treat major news as a boundary, not a challenge. I want to know when the market may become unusually unstable before I begin trading. If I am already emotional, that information becomes even more important.

Counselor's question: Are you trading the market you actually have, or the market you wish you had? If volatility changes the character of the market, your plan must be allowed to change with it.

Prop-Firm News Rules

Prop firms may impose specific restrictions around major economic releases.

Those rules vary.

Never rely on a generic internet rule.

Read the current rules of the specific program you are trading and understand whether the restriction applies before, during, or after an event and whether there are additional conditions.

The Professional Response

You do not have to trade every environment.

A professional trader knows when the environment does not match the strategy.

The market will offer another opportunity.

Your account may not survive the one you force.

Being Right Is Expensive

The market does not pay you for predicting correctly.

It pays according to your actual position, risk, and exit.

You can be directionally right and still lose.

You can be early and lose.

You can be late and win.

That is why prediction is not the complete game.

Moving the Stop

Moving a stop is often presented as patience.

Sometimes it is.

But when the only reason for moving the stop is that you cannot emotionally accept the loss, it is not patience.

It is refusal.

Define the invalidation point before the trade whenever possible.

Then respect it.

Changing Your Mind Is Strength

A professional can say:

"I was wrong."

That sentence does not destroy a trader.

The inability to say it can.

PART III — BUILDING A LIFE THAT SUPPORTS TRADING

The Best Time to Begin

One of the best times to begin learning futures trading is when you have a job, business, savings, or another reliable stream of income.

I want to be very clear about why.

When trading becomes responsible for your immediate survival, the psychological pressure changes.

A normal losing trade no longer feels like a normal business expense.

It feels like a threat.

You start thinking:

"I have to make money today."

"I need this payout."

"I cannot take another loss."

"I have to pass this evaluation."

That is when the market becomes an emotional emergency room.

Do Not Make the Market Your Emergency Fund

If the electricity bill is due Friday, that bill should not be depending on a Thursday morning futures trade.

If groceries need to be purchased, the market should not be responsible for making grocery money.

If your family needs stability, your trading account should not be carrying the emotional weight of providing that stability before you have proven that it can.

Trading can become an income stream.

But it should earn that responsibility through evidence.

One of the strongest lessons in my journey has been that trading becomes psychologically different when you need it to produce money immediately. A trade is no longer simply a probability. It becomes a solution to a problem. That is when patience becomes difficult.

If the rent, mortgage, groceries, or family obligations are mentally attached to today's trading result, a normal losing trade can feel like an emergency. The trader starts looking for another setup before the previous emotion has settled. Then size increases. Stops move. Rules become negotiable. The account becomes responsible for solving problems it was never designed to solve.

That is why I believe the best time to begin serious trading is while you still have a job, business, savings, or another reliable stream of income. Build the skill before you need the income. Develop your process while your survival does not depend on your next trade.

I also learned that researching other investment opportunities helped remove emotion from trading. When the market is one part of a broader financial plan, it does not have to carry the entire weight of your future. You can step away without feeling like you stepped away from your only chance.

Counselor's question: If you could not trade for thirty days, would your household still be financially okay? If not, the first trading goal may need to be building financial stability rather than increasing position size.

Income Gives You Time

A reliable income stream gives you the ability to wait.

You can take a loss.

You can stop for the day.

You can practice.

You can spend months learning.

You can say no to mediocre setups.

The trader who has time has a psychological advantage over the trader who needs the market to pay today.

From Need to Choice

The goal is to move from needing a trade to choosing a trade.

Need says, "This has to work."

Choice says, "This meets my criteria, and I accept the risk."

That difference is enormous.

The Stability Rule

Before increasing trading risk, ask whether your life can continue normally if trading produces no income this month.

If the answer is no, the solution may not be a better setup.

The solution may be strengthening your financial foundation first.

Trading Does Not Exist Alone

A trader can lose an account in an hour, but the emotional consequences can last all day.

That frustration can follow you into your home.

You may become quiet.

Irritable.

Distracted.

Preoccupied.

The people around you may not know what happened, but they

experience the person who walked away from the screen.

Do Not Make Your Family Pay for Your Trading Mistakes

Your spouse, children, family, and friends should not become emotional collateral for a bad trading day.

Create boundaries.

Set trading hours.

Set a time when the screens go off.

Do not spend every evening replaying trades.

Do not make your family responsible for calming you after losses.

Protect What Trading Cannot Replace

A trading account can be rebuilt.

Time with your children cannot be replayed.

A conversation with your spouse cannot always be postponed.

A peaceful home is worth more than another setup.

Trading should fit into your life—not consume the life you are trying to improve.

Life Has Already Taught You Something

Most adults have experienced some form of setback.

A job can change.

A plan can fail.

Someone can say no.

A season can end.

You can have to rebuild.

Those experiences can either make you more resilient or make you desperate to prove yourself.

Trading exposes which one you are carrying.

The Danger of Proving Yourself

After a major setback, trading can become a stage.

You want to prove you can still win.

You want to prove that the setback did not defeat you.

You want the account to become evidence that you are okay.

That is too much responsibility for a trading account.

Let your character carry that burden instead.

Rebuilding Slowly

When rebuilding after a blowup, reduce the size of the problem.

Do not immediately try to recover the money.

Recover the process first.

Recover sleep.

Recover discipline.

Recover the ability to stop.

Recover trust in yourself.

Then, and only then, rebuild the account.

The first stage of rebuilding is not about proving that you can make money. It is about proving that you can behave differently. A trader who has repeatedly blown accounts should not immediately return with the same size and the same expectations.

Start with observation. Study the market. Practice the setup. Use a simulator when appropriate. Build a journal. Learn the news schedule. Define the conditions that make you stop. Then move into small, controlled execution.

A recovery plan should be deliberately boring. The account may grow slowly. That is acceptable. The point is to create evidence that the new behavior can survive an ordinary losing day.

I also want the trader to build life outside the chart during this process. Work. Family. Exercise. Faith. Other investments. Rest. These are not distractions from becoming a better trader. They are part of becoming a person who can trade without making trading the center of everything.

Counselor's rule: Do not measure recovery only by dollars. Measure it by rule-following, emotional stability, controlled size, and the ability to walk away. Money is the lagging indicator.

Following Jesus Christ

I am a follower of Jesus Christ.

That is not a marketing line for me. It is part of how I understand who I am.

Faith shapes the way I think about money, responsibility, humility, patience, self-control, and how I treat people.

Trading cannot become my master.

Money cannot become my identity.

Success cannot become my god.

The goal is not to make trading a substitute for purpose. The goal is to become a disciplined person who can handle whatever level of success God allows.

Stewardship

Stewardship changes the question.

Instead of asking only, "How much can I make?"

You begin asking:

"How responsibly am I handling what I have?"

That includes capital.

Time.

Attention.

Relationships.

Opportunities.

A trader who protects capital is practicing stewardship.

Character Before Capital

If becoming profitable requires you to become dishonest, reckless, arrogant, or obsessed, the price is too high.

Money should serve your life.

It should not become the measure of your life.

Prayer and Preparation

For me, prayer is not a substitute for preparation.

I can pray and still study.

I can have faith and still use a stop.

I can trust God and still respect risk.

Faith does not remove responsibility.

It strengthens the way I carry it.

The mature trader therefore celebrates good decisions, not just green days. A profitable trade is welcome. A well-executed trade is repeatable. The long-term objective is to build behavior that can survive both outcomes.

Those observations are more valuable than a single winning screenshot. They turn trading from a collection of memories into a body of evidence.

Over time, the journal should reveal patterns. Maybe the trader performs well when waiting for confirmation but struggles when entering on anticipation. Maybe losses increase after two consecutive winners. Maybe the best trades occur during a particular session. Maybe the trader consistently gives back profits after reaching a certain daily number.

Review the trade in three layers. First, what did price do? Second, what did the plan say? Third, what did I actually do? The gap between those three answers is where much of the trader's improvement lives.

A professional process allows losing trades to exist without turning them into emergencies. The question is whether the loss occurred inside the expected distribution of the strategy and within the risk framework. One trade cannot answer whether a process works.

This distinction protects a trader from constantly changing strategies. Without it, every losing trade becomes evidence that the strategy is broken and every winning trade becomes evidence that the latest impulse was brilliant. The result is an endless cycle of strategy switching.

If the answers are strong and the trade lost, the lesson may be patience and sample size rather than strategy abandonment. If the answers are weak and the trade won, the lesson may be that the trader got rewarded for behavior that should not be repeated.

A useful post-trade review asks: Did I trade at a level I had identified in advance? Did the setup meet my criteria? Was the risk defined before entry? Did I know where the idea was invalidated? Did I follow the exit plan? Did I change anything because of fear, greed, or the desire to recover money?

This is why the trading journal should contain two separate scores: outcome and execution. Outcome records what happened financially. Execution records whether the trader followed the process. Both matter, but they answer different questions.

Now consider the opposite. A trader enters late without a setup, uses too much size, has no defined invalidation, and happens to catch a sudden move in his favor. The trade makes money. The outcome is profitable, but the behavior is dangerous because it teaches the trader that poor decisions work.

Suppose a trader identifies a clear level, waits for the planned condition, enters at the intended location, places the predetermined stop, and risks the correct amount. The market immediately reverses and stops the trade. That is a losing trade, but the decision may still have been good.

One of the hardest lessons in trading is that a good trade can lose and a bad trade can win. If you do not understand that distinction, your results can teach you the wrong lessons.

Profitable Trade

The goal is not to become slow. The goal is to become selective. When the right setup arrives, preparation should make action straightforward. Until then, doing nothing is not falling behind. It is protecting the opportunity to trade well later.

Patience is not a personality trait that some traders are born with. It is a behavior that can be trained. Every time you refuse a trade that does not meet your criteria, you reinforce the ability to wait. Every time you chase because you are afraid of missing out, you reinforce the opposite habit.

A useful question before every entry is: “If I were not already watching this chart, would this setup be good enough to make me open the platform?” If the answer is no, emotion may be driving the decision.

The discipline of waiting becomes easier when the trader has already defined what he is waiting for. Write the conditions down. Mark the levels. Decide what invalidates the idea. Decide what would make you stand aside. Then let the market come to you instead of chasing it.

Waiting also protects the trader from the emotional need to finish the day with a certain number of trades. A daily trade count is not a measure of productivity. Some days provide several high-quality opportunities. Some provide one. Some provide none. The trader's job is not to manufacture a quota.

False breakouts are especially useful teachers. Price can move through a level, attract participants, and then return through it. The trader who waits for confirmation may enter later, but he may also avoid reacting to the first burst of movement. There is no universal rule that every breakout requires confirmation; there should simply be a defined reason for the timing chosen.

Missed moves are another test of patience. Traders often feel that once price has moved without them, they must catch the remainder. That belief turns a completed opportunity into a new source of pressure. If the original entry is gone, it is gone. The next decision should be based on current structure, not regret about the previous candle.

One of the most important changes is learning to separate movement from opportunity. A large candle can be impressive without being tradable. A fast rally can be real without being an entry. A sharp reversal can happen without providing enough information to justify risk. The professional question is not, “Is the market moving?” It is, “Is the market giving me my setup?”

Waiting is different from being passive. A patient trader is actively observing. He knows where the important levels are, what would confirm the setup, what would invalidate it, and what conditions would make the trade unattractive. He is prepared to act when the market reaches his area because he did not spend the previous hour forcing trades.

The temptation to trade often begins with boredom. The screen is open, price is moving, and the trader starts looking for a reason to participate. A small movement becomes a setup. A weak level becomes important. A late entry begins to look like a breakout. The trader has not found an opportunity; he has created one because he wants to be involved.

Waiting is one of the least celebrated skills in trading and one of the most valuable. The market can move for hours without offering the exact conditions you need. A trader who has learned to wait does not experience that as punishment. He understands that inactivity can be part of the strategy.

PART IV — THE PROP-FIRM BATTLE

The Evaluation Mindset

The evaluation creates an artificial deadline in your mind.

You see the target.

You see the drawdown.

You start calculating how many days it will take.

Then you start increasing risk.

The target is not your trading plan.

Your trading plan is your trading plan.

A prop-firm account creates a unique psychological environment because the trader is operating inside a rule set that may include a profit target, daily loss limit, trailing drawdown, consistency requirements, and restrictions around certain events. Those rules are not minor details. They are the environment.

The mistake is treating the evaluation like a race. A trader sees the profit target and immediately asks how quickly it can be reached. That question encourages oversized positions and unnecessary frequency. A better question is, “How can I demonstrate that I can trade consistently enough to deserve the next stage?”

Passing is not the finish line. In many ways, it is the beginning of the real test. Once funded, the temptation can be to increase size because the account feels like an opportunity that must be maximized. The professional response is often the opposite: reduce risk, protect the account, and prove that consistency survives pressure.

Prop-firm rules also change over time and differ by company. Never assume that a rule described in a book, video, or social-media post is current. Read the firm's current terms before trading, especially regarding news, overnight positions, drawdown calculations, and payout requirements.

Counselor's exercise: Write every rule of your specific program on one page. Beside each rule, write the behavior that would cause you to violate it. Your job is to recognize the behavior before the violation happens.

Trade the Same Trader

Do not become aggressive because you are close to passing.

Do not suddenly double size.

Do not trade a setup you have never tested.

If your process is good enough to pass, let the process pass you.

The Goal Is Evidence

The best evaluation result is not merely a passed account.

It is evidence that you can operate within a defined risk structure.

That is what you will need after the evaluation.

Funded Is Different

Once funded, traders can become more emotional because the account feels real.

The temptation is to make up for all the time and effort spent passing.

That is precisely when you need to slow down.

Reduce Risk After Funding

A common psychological mistake is treating funding as permission to become aggressive.

Instead, consider funding permission to become more conservative.

You have something to protect now.

Risk management is where trading stops being a prediction game and becomes a survival game. You do not control whether the next trade wins. You can control how much damage a losing trade is allowed to do.

A useful risk plan has to account for more than account size. It should consider the stop distance, instrument volatility, contract value, maximum daily loss, trailing drawdown, and the trader's own emotional tolerance. A position that looks mathematically acceptable can still be psychologically too large.

The goal is not to eliminate losses. Losses are part of the business. The goal is to make losses ordinary enough that they do not trigger abnormal behavior. If one loss causes you to change your plan, the risk was probably too large.

Think of risk as buying the right to stay in the game. Every trade should leave enough capital and emotional capacity for the next opportunity.

Counselor's exercise: Write your maximum loss per trade and maximum loss per day before you trade. Then write what you will do after reaching each limit. The rule has to be decided while you are calm because you cannot depend on your future emotional self to negotiate responsibly.

The First Payout

A payout can create a dangerous thought:

"I figured it out."

No.

You produced one profitable period.

Celebrate it.

Then return to the process.

Consistency Before Scaling

Scale when your behavior proves you are ready.

Do not scale because your emotions are excited.

A larger position should feel as controlled as a smaller position.

If it does not, you have scaled too quickly.

Discipline becomes easier when it is designed into the day instead of demanded from yourself at the last second. A trader who waits until he is emotional to decide whether he will stop is asking emotion to enforce the rules that emotion already wants to break. The solution is to make important decisions before the market opens.

Write down the maximum number of trades. Write down the maximum daily loss. Write down the conditions that make a setup valid. Decide what will cause you to stop for the day. Then treat those decisions as commitments rather than suggestions.

I also believe discipline has to exist outside the trading platform. How you sleep, how you handle frustration, whether you keep promises to yourself, and whether you can delay gratification all influence what happens when money is moving quickly. Trading does not create character; it exposes it.

For me, faith belongs in this conversation because discipline is not just about getting what I want. It is also about stewardship. I want trading to fit underneath my responsibilities, not replace them. God comes first. Family matters. Work and obligations matter. Trading has a place, but it cannot become the center of my life.

Counselor's exercise: Pick one rule you repeatedly break and make it impossible to ignore. Put it beside your screen. Your goal is not to become perfect tomorrow. Your goal is to become more trustworthy to yourself.

Understanding the Psychological Drawdown

The drawdown number is not merely a financial boundary.

It becomes a psychological clock.

As you get closer, every trade feels larger.

That can create panic.

The solution is not to stare harder at the drawdown.

The solution is to define risk far enough away from the limit that normal variance cannot immediately threaten the account.

Your Personal Buffer

If the firm allows a certain maximum loss, do not automatically treat the full amount as money you are willing to risk.

Create your own internal limit.

Your internal limit should protect you from reaching the firm's limit.

Protect the Account From the Trader

The account is often not destroyed by the first loss.

It is destroyed by the trader's response to the first loss.

Build rules around the response.

Scaling Is a Psychological Event

More contracts do not simply mean more dollars.

They mean more emotional intensity.

If you double size, you may double the emotional significance of every tick.

That changes execution.

The Slow Ladder

Scale in small increments.

Measure performance at each level.

If behavior deteriorates, go back down.

There is no shame in reducing size.

The ability to reduce size is a sign of maturity.

Withdraw and Protect.

Prop-Firm Tactics: Read the rules, Read the price, Think for yourself

A Warning: "Tactics" Can Cut Both Ways

The Headline Account Is Not Your Real Risk

A program may advertise a large account balance, but that number is not necessarily the amount you can lose. The meaningful number is the actual drawdown boundary and how it is calculated. Before trading, know whether the boundary is static or trailing, whether unrealized gains affect it, how daily loss is measured, and what events can cause a violation.

The Evaluation Can Change Your Behavior

An evaluation creates a scoreboard. You know the target. You know the drawdown. You know there is a clock in your head. That can turn a normal setup into a perceived opportunity to "get closer." The trader begins trading the target instead of trading the market.

The Target Is Not a Signal

If you need $2,000 to pass, the next candle does not know that. If you are $300 from a payout, the market does not owe you $300. A target is an account objective, not technical confirmation. Let price create the setup and let the account rules determine whether the risk is acceptable.

Trailing Drawdown Can Create a Moving Psychological Ceiling

A trailing threshold can move upward as the account makes progress. The trader may feel safer because the account is profitable while simultaneously having less room than expected before a violation. Model the rule before trading. Know exactly where failure occurs under several realistic sequences.

Read the Rules Yourself

Never trade a prop-firm account from someone else's summary. Programs differ, rules change, and even similar terms can be calculated differently. Verify profit targets, daily loss, maximum drawdown, drawdown method, consistency requirements, news restrictions, trading hours, minimum days, and payout conditions directly from the current program rules.

The Real Product Is Discipline

The strongest evaluation result is not simply a passed account. It is evidence that you can repeatedly operate inside a defined risk framework. If passing required behavior you cannot maintain once funded, the pass did not solve the underlying problem.

Do Not Confuse an Indicator With the Market

Indicators can be useful, but they are measurements produced by formulas. They can use different sessions, feeds, settings, lookback periods, or definitions of the trading day. Two tools can produce different levels while both are mathematically correct according to their own inputs.

Draw Your Own Levels First

Before relying on automated support or resistance, mark what price itself has shown you: prior-session high and low, major swing points, opening range, gaps, consolidation boundaries, repeated rejection, and the origin of strong moves. The value of a manually drawn level is not that it is automatically correct. The value is that you can explain why it matters.

Indicators Are Assistants, Not Authorities

Draw the level first. Then compare the indicator. If the tool confirms the level, it can add context. If it disagrees, investigate the reason rather than moving your level simply to make the indicator right. The trader should be able to read a clean chart without surrendering judgment to an automated line.

One-Click Support and Resistance Can Hide the Important Question

An automated level may tell you where a calculation places support or resistance. It cannot necessarily tell you why price reacted there, whether the level is still relevant, or whether the market has accepted price beyond it. Human observation remains necessary.

Prop-Firm Rules and Price Levels Belong to Different Jobs

The firm determines what risk is permitted. Price determines whether the market setup exists. Do not let the account target create a trade, and do not let an account rule convince you that a bad price level is suddenly good. Separate the two decisions.

Protect Yourself From the Information Funnel

Countdowns, payout screenshots, promotions, automated signals, indicator packages, and social-media success stories can create urgency. You do not have to assume bad intent. You simply need to return to primary information: the current rules, the actual chart, your actual risk, and your actual trading record.

The Professional Response

The professional trader does not need to trade every condition. If the account structure, market environment, or emotional state does not fit the plan, waiting is a legitimate decision. The market will offer another opportunity. Your account may not survive the one you force.

Prop-Firm Level Checklist

- Previous session high and low
- Major swing highs and lows
- Opening range and important gaps
- Major consolidation boundaries
- Where the strongest move began
- Repeated rejection or acceptance areas
- Levels visible without indicators
- Whether the current session respects those levels
- Whether the indicator agrees with the price-based level
- What data or calculation explains disagreement
- Where the setup is invalidated

• Whether the position fits the actual drawdown mechanics

When the program permits it and your financial plan supports it, consider taking profits rather than endlessly increasing exposure.

The goal of scaling should be to improve your financial position, not to create a larger number on a screen.

PART V — THE TRADING COUNSELOR

Trigger One: Loss

Loss can trigger anger, fear, shame, and urgency.

Do not wait until those emotions are extreme.

Identify your earliest signal.

Maybe you sit forward.

Maybe your breathing changes.

Maybe you start clicking faster.

Maybe you stop writing in your journal.

That is your warning.

Trigger Two: Missing the Move

FOMO is often grief disguised as opportunity.

You watched the move happen without you.

Now you want to participate after the best entry has passed.

Ask:

"Would I enter here if I had not just watched the move?"

If the answer is no, wait.

Trigger Three: Winning

Winning can trigger overconfidence.

You feel invincible.

Your standards loosen.

Your size increases.

The best defense is a winning-day protocol.

Trigger Four: Financial Pressure

If you are thinking about bills while trading, your risk tolerance may not be objective.

This is why stable income and a financial buffer are so important.

A trader who needs today's trade to work is not making the same decision as a trader who can walk away.

Why It Works

The reset creates separation between emotion and action.

You are not trying to eliminate emotion.

You are trying to prevent emotion from becoming an order.

The Full Reset

Step one: Close the platform.

Step two: Stand up.

Step three: Walk for five minutes.

Step four: Drink water.

Step five: Slow your breathing.

Step six: Write what happened without blaming the market.

Step seven: Identify the rule that was followed or broken.

Step eight: Ask whether you are calm enough to return.

If not, the session is over.

The Sentence

Use this sentence:

"This loss is data, not identity."

Then add:

"I do not have to recover it today."

Those words matter because revenge trading begins with urgency.

Why Winning Can Be Dangerous

A trader can become reckless after success because success temporarily removes fear.

Fear had kept the trader small.

Now confidence removes the brakes.

This is why a winning-day protocol is essential.

The Protocol

When you hit your daily objective:

Screenshot the session.

Record what worked.

Record what did not.

If you choose to continue trading under your written plan, do so only if the plan explicitly allows it and the risk remains unchanged.

Do not improvise because you feel good.

Walking Away Is a Trade

Closing the platform is an active decision.

You are choosing not to expose capital to another uncertain outcome.

You are protecting tomorrow's opportunity.

When the Session Is Over

Stop when:

Your maximum loss is reached.

Your maximum number of trades is reached.

Your daily objective is reached, if that is part of your plan.

You notice emotional escalation.

Market conditions no longer fit your strategy.

You are tired, distracted, or mentally compromised.

Do Not Immediately Buy Another Challenge

The emotional impulse after losing an account is often to replace it.

That may be the worst possible next step.

Pause.

Study the account.

Find the first rule violation.

Find the first emotional decision.

Find the moment when risk changed.

The 72-Hour Rule

Consider creating a personal rule that you do not immediately restart after a major blowup.

Use the time to review.

Journal.

Talk to someone you trust.

Then decide what needs to change before money goes back on the line.

Rebuilding Trust

You do not rebuild trust by promising.

You rebuild it by collecting evidence.

One disciplined session.

Then another.

Confidence should be earned from behavior.

PART VI — BUILDING THE PROFESSIONAL

The Sniper

The Sniper waits for a small number of high-quality setups.

Strength: patience.

Risk: frustration during inactivity.

The Sniper must learn that missing trades is normal.

A strategy becomes useful only when it can be executed consistently under pressure. A beautiful setup on a chart is not enough. The trader needs a defined environment, an entry condition, an invalidation point, a target or exit plan, and a clear reason not to trade.

This is where personality matters. A trader who hates sitting still may struggle with a strategy that produces only one setup a day. A trader who becomes anxious with fast price movement may not belong in a rapid-fire scalping approach. A trader who wants constant confirmation may miss the very move his strategy was designed to capture.

I would rather have a simple strategy I can execute correctly than a complicated strategy that looks impressive but collapses when my emotions rise. The strategy should reduce decisions, not create more of them.

Backtesting and journaling are also essential because they separate what we believe from what the data shows. A setup that feels powerful may have a very different performance profile when reviewed across dozens or hundreds of examples.

Counselor's question: Could you explain your setup to another trader in less than two minutes, including exactly when you will not take it? If you cannot, your system may still be an idea rather than a strategy.

The Scalper

The Scalper thrives on fast decisions.

Strength: speed.

Risk: overtrading.

The Scalper needs strict limits and clear stop conditions.

The Intraday Swing Trader

This trader holds longer and allows more room.

Risk: interfering with trades because of short-term noise.

The key is trust in tested structure.

The Liquidity Hunter

This trader looks for sweeps, stop runs, and reversals.

Strength: awareness of market behavior.

Risk: seeing liquidity everywhere.

The solution is objective criteria.

Build Around Yourself

Do not build a strategy for the trader you wish you were.

Build one for the trader you actually are—and then gradually develop the person you want to become.

Entry

Define exactly what must be present before entry.

If you cannot explain the setup to another person, it may not be defined enough.

Risk

Define maximum dollar risk.

Define stop placement.

Define maximum contracts.

Define daily loss.

Define maximum consecutive losses.

Exit

Define profit-taking.

Define invalidation.

Define what you will do if price stalls.

Define whether you use trailing management or fixed targets.

Time

Define the sessions you trade.

Define when you do not trade.

Do not allow the market's availability to become your schedule.

News

Define the events you avoid.

Verify current prop-firm rules.

Do not improvise around high-impact releases.

Mental State

Define when you are not allowed to trade.

Examples:

Severe fatigue.

Significant emotional distress.

Major distraction.

Financial desperation.

Compulsion to recover losses.

The trader sitting in front of the screen is still a whole person. Sleep, stress, family conflict, financial pressure, confidence, fatigue, and unresolved frustration all come into the room with you. Pretending they do not exist does not make them disappear.

That is why emotional hygiene is part of risk management. If I slept poorly, feel unusually angry, am distracted by a family problem, or am desperate to make money today, those conditions matter. The professional response may be to reduce size or not trade at all.

I also learned that stepping away can be productive. During my own resets I prayed, spent time with family, exercised, reflected, and researched other investment opportunities. Those activities helped remove trading from the center of my attention. When I returned, the chart was still there, but I was no longer demanding that it fix my emotions.

If trading begins interfering with sleep, relationships, work, or daily functioning, that deserves serious attention. A trusted mental-health professional can be a valuable part of a trader's support system. There is no shame in getting help before a pattern becomes destructive.

Counselor's question: What does your body feel like immediately before you break a trading rule? Learn those signals. Your body may warn you before your conscious mind admits that you are in danger.

Morning

Start before the market.

Pray and reflect.

Review your purpose.

Check your schedule.

Check the economic calendar.

Mark levels.

Define risk.

Visualize both outcomes.

During Trading

Slow down.

Breathe.

Read the plan.

Wait for the setup.

Execute.

Accept the outcome.

Do not negotiate with yourself after entry.

After Trading

Close the platform.

Grade the process.

Record emotional triggers.

Celebrate discipline.

Leave the market behind.

Days 1–30: Stabilize

Use simulation or minimal appropriate risk.

Your goal is not profit.

Your goal is behavioral stability.

Learn your triggers.

Build the routine.

Study one market.

Study one setup family.

Days 31–60: Prove Repeatability

Measure your best setups.

Measure your worst habits.

Identify your most dangerous time of day.

Identify what happens after wins and losses.

Build rules around those patterns.

Days 61–90: Controlled Pressure

If you begin an evaluation, keep your process intact.

Do not speed up.

Do not increase risk because you are close.

Treat the evaluation as a demonstration of discipline.

The Real 90-Day Score

At the end of 90 days, do not ask only how much money you made.

Did I reduce impulsive trades?

Did I respect risk?

Did I stop more easily?

Did I improve my emotional awareness?

Did I reduce financial pressure?

Did I become more consistent?

Those are the foundations of a professional.

The Rules

I will not use trading as an emergency source of income.

I will not risk money required for essential living expenses.

I will not increase size because I am angry.

I will not trade to recover pride.

I will not chase a move because I missed it.

I will not violate my account rules because I believe the trade will win.

I will stop when my written conditions say stop.

I will protect time away from the market.

I will review my behavior honestly.

I will choose consistency over excitement.

I will remember that my identity is larger than my P&L.

I will seek wisdom and support when I need it.

I will practice self-control.

I will give myself time to grow.

I will not allow one trade to become responsible for my future.

The Conversation After the Worst Day

If I could sit across from you after your worst trading day, I would not begin by asking how much you lost.

I would ask:

What happened before the loss?

What were you feeling?

What pressure were you carrying?

When did the plan disappear?

What did you know you should do but refused to do?

Then I would tell you:

You do not have to fix everything today.

You do not have to recover everything today.

You do not have to prove anything today.

You need to stop the pattern.

Once the pattern stops, you can build.

The New Identity

You are not the trader who has to chase every move.

You are not the trader who has to get the lick back.

You are not the trader who needs one trade to rescue the day.

You are the trader who can wait.

You are the trader who can take a loss.

You are the trader who can stop.

You are the trader who can protect the account.

You are the trader who understands that discipline is not a mood.

It is a practice.

The Final Lesson

Trading is not a battle against the market.

It is a confrontation with the parts of yourself that want immediate answers.

Impatience.

Ego.

Fear.

Greed.

Pride.

Desperation.

The need to prove something.

The need to recover.

You do not defeat those emotions by pretending they do not exist.

You learn to recognize them before they become behavior.

A Word of Faith

As a follower of Jesus Christ, I believe my life is larger than a trading account.

That belief changes how I approach success.

I can pursue excellence without worshiping money.

I can pursue growth without making profit my identity.

I can accept correction.

I can practice discipline.

I can be grateful.

I can begin again.

The goal is not simply to become a profitable trader.

The goal is to become a person capable of handling success without losing yourself.

Your Turning Point

If you have blown accounts, let the past become information.

Not an identity.

Not a sentence.

Information.

Study it.

Learn from it.

Build rules around it.

Then move forward.

Trade smaller.

Trade slower.

Protect your income.

Protect your relationships.

Protect your mind.

Protect your character.

Master your mind.

Protect your capital.

Respect the process.

Become the trader you meant to be.

Personal Trading Constitution

I will not use the market as an emergency source of income.

I will not risk money I cannot afford to lose.

I will not increase size after a loss.

I will not chase.

I will not trade major news unless my tested plan and account rules explicitly permit it.

I will respect my stop.

I will respect my daily loss limit.

I will stop when my plan says stop.

I will protect my time, family, health, and peace.

I will seek wisdom when I need it.

I will remember that my identity is not my P&L.

I will keep God first.

I will seek wisdom before action.

I will measure success by discipline, not excitement.

I will accept that some days the best trade is no trade.

I will remember that tomorrow is another opportunity.

Signed: ______________________________

Date: ________________________________

FINAL WORD FROM THE COUNSELOR

If you remember only one thing from this book, remember this:

The market is not your enemy.

Your emotions are not your enemy either.

They are signals.

Fear tells you something matters.

Greed tells you you may want too much.

Anger tells you something hurt.

Urgency tells you you are trying to force time.

The professional trader learns to hear those signals without obeying them.

You may still have losing days.

You may still make mistakes.

You may still have moments when you want to get your lick back.

The difference is what you do next.

Take the break.

Get back to your life.

Come back tomorrow.

Start small.

Trade the plan.

And remember why you wanted trading in the first place.

It was supposed to give you freedom.

Don't become a prisoner of the thing you hoped would set you free.

Keep God first.

Protect your family.

And when you need a reminder, open this book again.

— Chris Lloyd

APPENDIX — WORKBOOK

Daily Pre-Market Checklist

Sleep quality: __________

Mood: calm / neutral / anxious / excited / angry

News scheduled today: __________

Key levels: __________

Primary setup: __________

Secondary setup: __________

Maximum trades: __________

Maximum consecutive losses: __________

Am I trading because I see an opportunity or because I need money? __________

The purpose of a journal is not to create paperwork. It is to create evidence. Memory is unreliable after a stressful trading day. A trader remembers the big win, the painful loss, the trade that almost worked, and the opportunity that was missed. A written record reveals the pattern underneath all of those stories.

Record the setup, size, stop, target, time, result, and emotional state. Then add one sentence about whether you followed your rules. That last question can be more valuable than the P&L.

Over several weeks, patterns begin to emerge. Maybe losses cluster around a particular time of day. Maybe your best trades occur after waiting fifteen minutes. Maybe your largest losses happen after your first losing trade. Maybe your size increases after a win. Those patterns are actionable.

Review should be curious rather than punitive. The purpose is not to call yourself stupid. The purpose is to discover the behavior that needs to change.

Counselor's exercise: At the end of each week, identify one behavior to keep, one behavior to stop, and one behavior to test. Improvement becomes much easier when you work on one behavior at a time.

The Financial Pressure Check

Do I need today's trading profits to pay an immediate bill?

Am I depending on a payout that has not been earned?

Would I make this trade if my immediate financial obligations were already covered?

Am I trying to make today's market solve a problem that should be solved outside the market?

If financial pressure is affecting my decisions, what is the responsible action? __________

Trade Journal

Date / Time: __________

Instrument: __________

Session: __________

Setup type: __________

Entry: __________

Stop: __________

Target: __________

Contracts: __________

Dollar risk: __________

Outcome: Win / Loss / Break-even

P&L: __________

Emotion before: __________

Emotion during: __________

Emotion after: __________

Did I follow the plan? Yes / No

Did I move my stop? Yes / No

Did I add size? Yes / No

Did I chase? Yes / No

Did I revenge trade? Yes / No

Lesson learned: __________

Weekly Review

What did I do well?

What did I do poorly?

What emotion appeared most often?

What rule did I break?

What behavior made me money?

What behavior cost me money?

Did I overtrade?

Did I oversize?

Did I stop when I said I would?

Did I protect my relationships?

What is one behavior I will improve next week?

1. Close the platform.
2. Stand up.
3. Walk for five minutes.
4. Drink water.
5. Breathe slowly.
6. Write the facts of the trade.
7. Write: "This loss is data, not identity."
8. Write: "I do not have to recover this today."
9. Ask whether the next trade would exist if the previous trade had never happened.
10. Return only if calm.

If you are not calm, the session is over.

Winning-Day Protocol

When you reach your daily objective:

Journal the process.

Record the emotional state.

Ask whether continuing is part of your written plan.

If continuing is not explicitly planned, close the platform.

Protect the green day.

Loss-Day Protocol

When your maximum loss is reached:

Do not increase size.

Do not buy another evaluation immediately.

Do not search for a miracle setup.

Do not blame the market.

Review the sequence later when calm.

Tomorrow is another session.

Prop-Firm Rules Verification

Firm: ___________

Program: ___________

Profit target: ___________

Daily loss rule: ___________

Maximum drawdown: ___________

Drawdown method: static / trailing / other

Consistency requirement: ___________

News restrictions: ___________

Trading-hour restrictions: ___________

Minimum trading days: ___________

Payout requirements: ___________

Date rules were last verified: ___________

Never rely on memory when an account's rules determine whether the account survives.

not my P&L.

BLOWN ACCOUNT RECOVERY PLAN

If I blow an account or experience a major trading loss:

1. Stop trading immediately.
2. Close the platform.
3. Do not open another evaluation to immediately recover the loss.
4. Take at least the amount of time necessary for the revenge and urgency to leave.
5. Pray and reconnect with God.
6. Spend time with family and return to normal life.
7. Sleep and exercise.

8. Review the trades only after emotions have settled.

9. Identify the behavior that caused the failure.

10. Research other investment or income opportunities so trading does not feel like my only path forward.

11. Rebuild the plan.

12. Reduce size dramatically when returning.

13. Treat the next session like a new account.

14. Focus on execution, not recovery speed.

15. Do not attempt to win back the entire loss in one day.

The purpose of this plan is not to erase the loss. The purpose is to prevent one loss from becoming a pattern of losses.

www.ingramcontent.com/pod-product-compliance
Lightning Source LLC
LaVergne TN
LVHW021737071126
851857LV00040B/1556
* 9 7 9 8 2 3 4 1 9 1 3 0 4 *